Jack and the Beanstalk a Pantomime

abridged by Christine Hall and Martin Coles

Pantomimes are usually put on at Christmas time. The main male character, (like Jack), is usually acted by a young woman. The old woman character is usually acted by a man. Often two people make up the front and back of the cow. Pantomimes should be fun, with lots of singing and dancing and shouting – and a happy ending for the main characters.

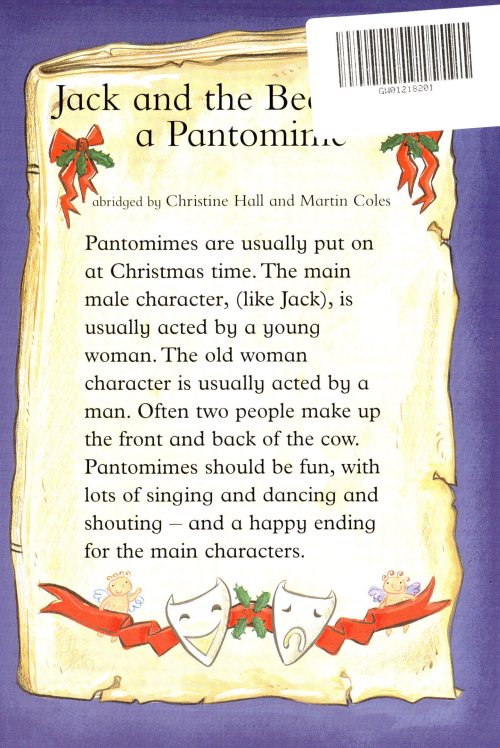

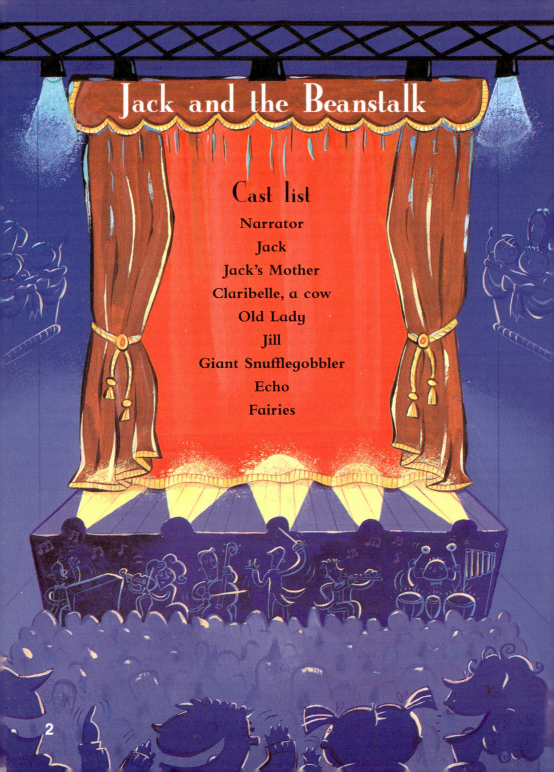

Act 1 Scene 1 — Jack and the Beanstalk – a Pantomime — STALLS

Scenes and settings

Act 1   Prologue
          Scene 1   On the road to market, in the morning
          Scene 2   In the cottage garden, in the afternoon

Act 2   Prologue
          Scene 1   On the road to the giant's castle, the next morning outside the giants castle
          Scene 2   One hour later, in the kitchen of the giant's castle
          Scene 3   Two hours later, on the road from the giant's castle

Act 3   Scene 1   In the cottage garden, later that day
          Scene 2   In the cottage garden, even later that day

Act 1 Prologue

NARRATOR My friends, you are welcome! Enjoy the show!
In this short panto, you'll soon get to know
Young Jack and his mother, really quite well.
And their family cow, dear Claribelle.
But when we first meet them, right at the start,
The cow and the family just have to part,
For Jack and his mother can't pay the rent;
All of their money for food has been spent.
Sadly they see they must sell their dear cow
And Jack's off to town, to do that right now.

Scene 1

The road to market. Jack comes in with Claribelle

JACK Oh, it is hot. Come on, Claribelle – only another five miles.

COW Moo…oo…oo.

JACK Poor old girl. It *is* a shame to sell you after all these years. Do you mind *very* much?

COW Moo…oo.

JACK I hope we can find a good home for you.

I want to sell you to someone who will treat you well.

COW *(in tears)* Moo…oo…oo.

JACK	Oh Claribelle darling, don't cry! You make me feel so mean. I know it's my fault that we've got to sell you. It's all my fault. Oh! I know I'm lazy and stupid and mean. I'm no good at all.
COW *(shakes head)*	Moo…moo…moo! Moo! Moo! Moo!
JACK *(kisses cow)*	You old darling. What a darling cow you are!

Old Lady comes in and sits down

JACK	Oh! You must think I'm silly kissing a cow… You look tired. Have you come far?

Act 1 Scene 1 — Jack and the Beanstalk – a Pantomime STALLS

OLD LADY	Yes, a long way.
JACK	In this heat? You must be worn out.
OLD LADY	I am. But I've got to get to town soon or I won't get work.
JACK	Work? Do you have to work?
OLD LADY	If I don't work, I don't eat.
JACK	Haven't you got any money?
OLD LADY	Nothing.
JACK	Oh! Here, take this twopence. It's all I've got.
OLD LADY	No. Oh, no! I couldn't do that.
JACK	Please! I wish I could give you more but it's all I have …
To himself	
	Except Claribelle …
Thinks	
	Yes – yes …
To Old Lady	
	You can have Claribelle.
OLD LADY	Claribelle?
JACK	The cow.

OLD LADY	Oh, my dear, it's so kind of you. But what will your mother say when you get back?
JACK	I'll explain it to her. She'll understand. Won't she, Claribelle?
COW (nods head)	Moo!
OLD LADY	Then I'll take her, dear boy. But I must give you something.

She gives Jack a small bag

Here, this is for you, with all my thanks.

JACK   Why – thank you.

He looks inside

Some beans! I can't take these.

OLD LADY	Yes, yes, you must!
JACK	Well, thank you.
OLD LADY	Now I will get on my way.
	You are a good boy.
	Look after my gift and you'll find your heart's desire.
	Don't forget me. Goodbye!
Old Lady leaves	
JACK	Goodbye!… What a funny lady!
	Beans! Mother won't like this!

Scene 2

The cottage garden

MOTHER How much longer will Jack be? It's time he was back. I wonder how much he got for her?

Poor Claribelle!

Jack tiptoes up behind her and puts one hand over her eyes. She screams

Oh – oh – who is it?

JACK I'll give you one guess, mother.

MOTHER Jack! I'm so glad you're back.

She sees the bag

Oh! Did you get a lot of money for Claribelle? There must be a lot of money in that bag.

Jack, my darling, my clever, clever darling!

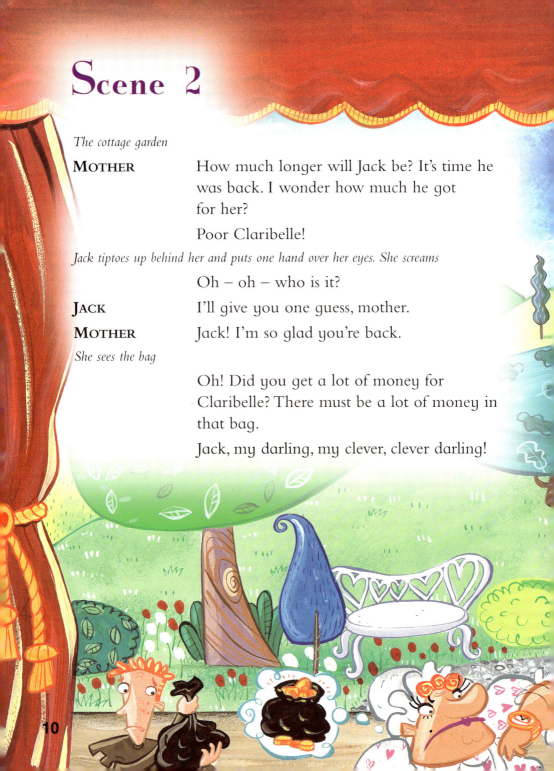

JACK	But, mother, listen…

Mother does not listen to him and takes the bag

MOTHER	I've never had so much money in my hands before.
JACK	Mother! Mother!

Mother opens the bag and puts her hand in

MOTHER	What's this? What's this?
JACK	B-b-b-beans, mother!
MOTHER	Beans? **Beans?** BEANS? Ooh-er!

She starts to cry

JACK	I'm sorry, so sorry, mother. I didn't think.

MOTHER	Think? Didn't think? You haven't got anything to think *with*! Beans! Bah!

Throws the beans over the garden

> There go your beans and you can go with them! Never let me see your face again.

She goes into the cottage and slams the door. Jack knocks on the door

JACK	Mother, mother, let me in… Please, oh please.

Knocks again

> Oh, mother – mother! Mother! Mother, let me in! Oh, do let me in – I'm so sorry, really I am…

MOTHER	You're not coming in here! You can stop out all night!
JACK	Mother – I'm sorry…
MOTHER	Go AWAY! Go a long way **AWAY!**
JACK	I might as well.

Turning away

> Oh, isn't it terrible? No money – no Claribelle – no bed – no dinner…Oh-o-oh!

He lies down, crying. Soon he falls asleep. Some fairies come in and dance round him as he sleeps

Dance of the fairies

The Beanstalk starts to grow

Act 2 Prologue

NARRATOR

Jack's dreams were terrible all through the night.
When he awoke in the bright morning light
His mouth fell open; he blinked both his eyes,
He could not believe the beanstalk's huge size!
All the night long, the stalk had been growing,
Growing and growing, going and going!
Jack climbed up the beanstalk. He did not stop.
What did he find when he got to the top?
A magical land! He jumped off the stalk.
Now for adventure! He started to walk…

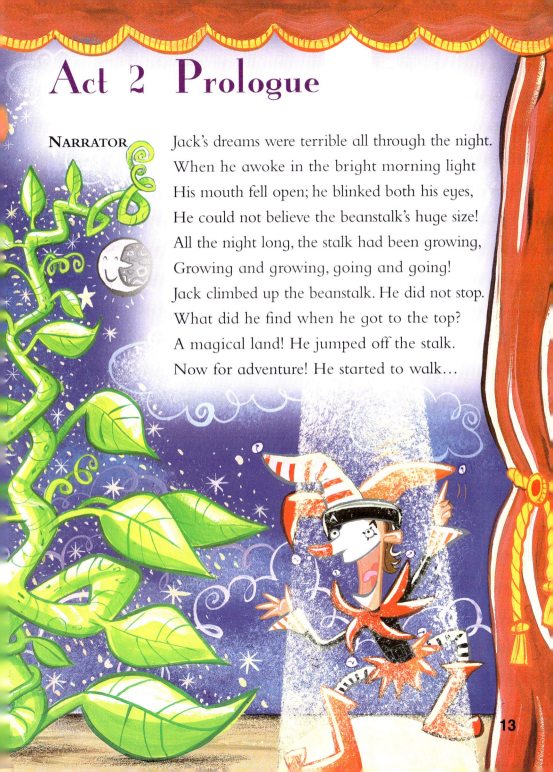

Scene 1

At the top of the beanstalk, on the road to the castle. The fairies come in first, dancing. Jack follows them but he can't see them. The fairies leave after their dance

JACK What a place! There's something funny about it! I feel as if there are people all round me – but there's no one! This isn't an adventure after all. I'm tired and hungry.

Gets up and shouts

Hey! Anyone round here?

ECHO …round here?

JACK Round where?

ECHO …'dwhere!

JACK *(shouting)* I want some *dinner*!

ECHO …some dinner!

JACK Don't keep repeating – it's so *rude*!

ECHO RU-U-U-U-U-U-de!

Clap of thunder

JACK *(afraid)* That's done it! I'm off! I'm going home!

ECHO Ho…me!

Act 2 Scene 1 — Jack and the Beanstalk – a Pantomime

Old Lady comes in

OLD LADY   No! Don't do that!

JACK   What!

OLD LADY   I say – don't – do – *that!*

JACK   Why! You're the old lady who had Claribelle, aren't you?

How did you get here?

OLD LADY   I'm all over the place. I'm never far away from anywhere!

JACK   I wish I was far from here. I thought I'd find adventure, but I've just found funny noises. I'm going home!

OLD LADY   And I – said – no! I don't want to see you give in, after I've helped you this far!

JACK   You *helped* me get here?

OLD LADY   Well, you climbed my beanstalk, didn't you?

JACK   Oh yes! It was a giant beanstalk!

OLD LADY   Giant! You might well say that! You do know where you are, do you?

Jack	N–no!
Old Lady	You're in the Land of the Giant Snufflegobbler.
Jack	Snufflegobbler? Never heard of him!
Old Lady	That's his castle over there.
	You'll find all the adventure you want there!
	Oh yes – all the adventure you want! Think of it! A real giant!
Jack	Oh – er – really? Is it safe?
Old Lady	Safe! Is any adventure safe? Are you afraid?
Jack	Yes – but – I'm going –

Old Lady leaves

I know – I must go!

But will you tell me…goodness! She's gone!

And I must go too! To the giant's castle! And my adventure!

Jack leaves

Scene 2

The kitchen of Giant Snufflegobbler's castle

JACK *(off)*   Is anyone there?…

Knocks

                       Can I come in?

Jack comes in

                       Well… I'm *in*! Anyone at home?… What a funny place. I don't like this at all. Gosh! What's that? Th-th-the giant? I'd better hide.

He hides behind door. Jill comes in carrying a cloth. She puts it on the table

Jack peeps out

                       It's a girl… It's a beautiful girl! *She* can't hurt me!

                       Er – excuse me – er –

JILL *(afraid)*   Oh… Oh… Who are you? What are you doing here?

JACK	I've lost my way and I'm hungry. So when I saw this castle, I decided to ask for something to eat and drink, and to find out where I was.
JILL	But you can't stay here. Don't you know who lives here?
JACK	Who?
JILL	Giant Snufflegobbler!
JACK	Oh yes – I've heard of him! Well? What about it? Wouldn't he give me something to eat?
JILL	Yes. He'd give you lots to eat for a week or so…
JACK	That sounds all right!
JILL	… and then…
JACK	And then?
JILL	He – he'd eat you himself!
JACK	Eat me? Why?
JILL	He eats boys and girls.
JACK	I don't think I'll like him, somehow. Why hasn't he eaten *you*?

JILL	He says I'm too thin.
JACK	Thin? You're not. I think you're just right.
JILL	Do you?
JACK	I think you're *lovely*!
JILL	Do you really? What does "lovely" mean?
JACK	Well – er – it's sort of – um – er… What's your name?
JILL	Jill.
JACK	Jill what?
JILL	I don't know.
JACK	That's strange.
JILL	Not really. You see, when I was about four the Giant stole me. I was too young to remember my name.
JACK	Then how do you know your name is Jill?
JILL	Because when I was stolen I had a brooch on my dress and I've still got it. See, it has my name on it.
JACK	Jill… and a crown above it!
	Anyway, I'm not going *now*!
JILL	But you *mustn't* stay! The giant will be here for dinner soon.
JACK	You can't send me away without anything to eat!
JILL	I must! I tell you, he'll eat you if he catches you.

JACK	Jill! Please! Be a darling…
JILL	*(smiles)* All right then. But we must hurry. Er – what is *your* name?
JACK	Jack.
JILL	And your other name?
JACK *(cheekily)*	You can call me darling!
JILL	Very well, Jack. Darling!
JACK	That sounded good!
JILL	Oh, did it?… What does it mean?
JACK	Oh! I thought you knew… It means… It means that you like me.
JILL	Now you must be gone before the Giant returns. Come on, Jack…

Noises off. Giant is coming

Oh no! He's coming! It's the giant! He's coming!

Hide… Oh hide… Under the table, Jack…

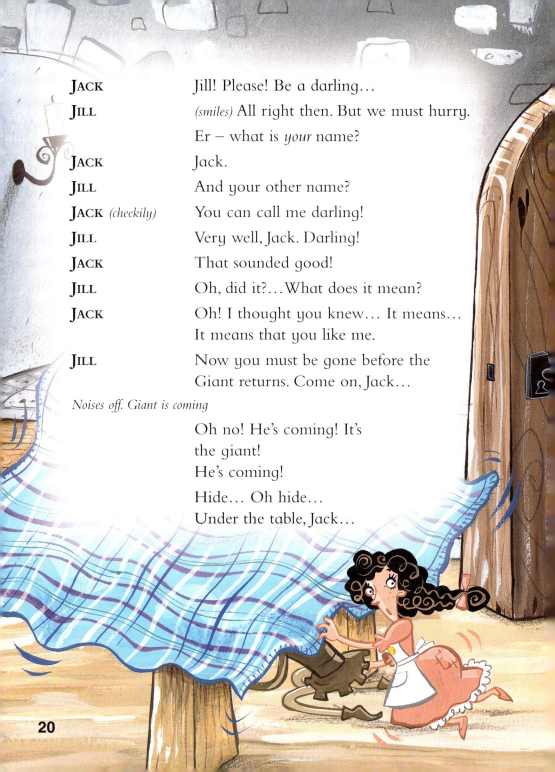

Jack hides under the table hidden by the tablecloth

GIANT   Fee - fi - fo - fum!

JILL *(to Jack)*   Are you all right under there?

GIANT   Fee - fi - fo - fum!

Giant comes in

GIANT *(singing)*   Fee - fi - fo - fum!
I smell the blood of an Englishman!
Be he live or be he dead
I'll grind his bones to make my bread!
Fee - fi - fo - fum!
Where is he, I say?

JILL   There's no one here, master. You can smell the lovely stew that I am cooking for dinner.

GIANT   Stew? Stew! Bah! I smell a human!

Tablecloth trembles

JILL	Oh, no, it must be the stew, master.
GIANT	Ah...ah... It may be so. I am very, very hungry indeed.

Tablecloth trembles. Jack groans

GIANT	What was that noise?
JILL	It was only the wind in the trees, master.
GIANT	Ah... My nerves are upset by this strange smell.
	Bring my money bags to make me feel better.

Jill brings money bags. Giant looks at his money

GIANT	Lovely... lovely... my beautiful treasure!
	Put this away. Now bring me the hen that lays the golden eggs.
JILL	Yes, master.

Jill brings hen to the Giant

GIANT	My treasure! Oh, bird beyond all price, lay me one of your golden eggs.

The hen lays a golden egg

Ha – ha! Beautiful! But I still feel strange.
This smell makes me restless.
There is a stranger about.

Cloth trembles again

I'll walk outside and find that stranger.

Giant goes out

JILL	Come out, Jack! Come out! You must leave now!

Jack comes out from under the table

JACK	Oh, Jill!
JILL	Oh hurry! You must hurry!
JACK	But aren't you coming with me?
JILL	No. I can't run very fast and he would catch us if I came with you. No… You go… quickly!
JACK	I'm not going without you! You must come!
JILL	But if I do, I'll have no home or friends to go to.
JACK	I'll be your friend for as long as I live. And as for a home… why don't you share my home with me?
JILL	Oh, yes! I'd love to be your servant!
JACK	Servant! Servant? I'm not asking you to be my servant! No, I'm asking you to be my wife!
JILL	Your wife! Oh! How lovely… Oh, Jack, darling…

They look dreamily at one another. Music

Act 2 Scene 2 — Jack and the Beanstalk – a Pantomime STALLS

Jill suddenly remembers where they are

JILL Come on! We need to get out of here!

Jack takes the money bags. Jill takes the hen. They leave, running. Giant comes in

GIANT They've stolen my hen! They've stolen my money!

Thieves! Robbers!

I'll have you alive, or I'll have you **dead!** And grind your **bones** to make my **bread!**

Giant goes out, roaring

Scene 3

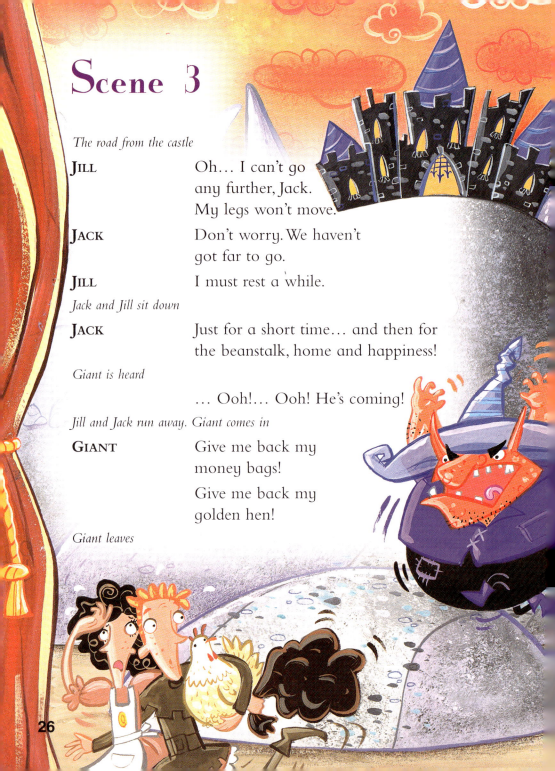

The road from the castle

JILL   Oh… I can't go any further, Jack. My legs won't move.

JACK   Don't worry. We haven't got far to go.

JILL   I must rest a while.

Jack and Jill sit down

JACK   Just for a short time… and then for the beanstalk, home and happiness!

Giant is heard

     … Ooh!… Ooh! He's coming!

Jill and Jack run away. Giant comes in

GIANT   Give me back my money bags!

     Give me back my golden hen!

Giant leaves

Act 3 Scene 1

The cottage garden

MOTHER Oh dear. It's terrible without Jack. He was a bad lad but I do miss him. I blame that beanstalk. If it hadn't been there, Jack would still be with me. Curse the thing. I'll chop the stupid thing down!

Gets axe and starts chopping

This is the end of you. You *(chop)* vile *(chop)* vegetable *(chop)*. There's one for me *(chop)* and one for Jack *(chop)*

She hears a shout

JACK Hey! Oy! Stop it! Stop that chopping!

MOTHER It's Jack! It's Jack! Where are you, my darling boy?

JACK Coming down!

Just a minute, mother, there's someone else coming.

Jill comes down

MOTHER	Who is she?
JACK	Mother! Meet my future wife!
MOTHER	But what do you know about her?
JACK	I know that her name is Jill. I know I saved her from Giant Snufflegobbler. And I know that we love each other.
MOTHER	Jill! Giant Snufflegobbler! Never heard of him! How do you know that her name is Jill?
JILL	I have a brooch with my name on. See!
MOTHER	"Jill", and a crown! Why you…

She does a curtsey

	Jack, you can't marry her.
JACK AND JILL	Why not?
MOTHER	Well – er – you are – you haven't – you haven't got any money…

Jack drops the money bag

JACK	Wrong! There's lots of money now!

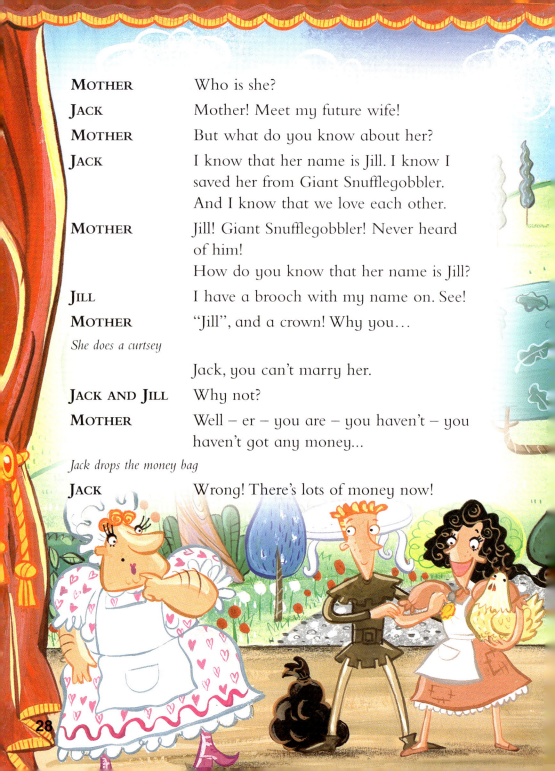

Act 3 Scene 1 — Jack and the Beanstalk – a Pantomime — STALLS

Noise of Giant coming down the beanstalk

JACK   It's the Giant! He's coming down here!

JILL   What shall we do? He's coming!

Giant roars

JACK   The axe, Mother! Where did you put the axe?

They chop down the beanstalk

JACK   It's all over. Giant Snufflegobbler is dead. Don't be afraid.

Mother, Jill! I'm so happy!

JILL   Jack! Mother! I'm so happy too!

MOTHER *(crying)*   Jack! Jill! Oh… oh… I'm so happy too!

JACK   This happiness is all too much for me!

Come on Jill! Let's go and see if we can make this our wedding day!

They leave

Scene 2

Cottage garden. Mother and fairies come in first, happily. Then Jack, in fine clothes, and Jill in a princess's dress

JILL Dear friends, please give us your good wishes!

JACK Yes, Mother, give us your blessing.

The King has already given us *his* blessing.

MOTHER The King?

JACK Yes, for Jill is the King's daughter.

She was stolen by the giant when she was very young.

JILL A man in town saw my brooch and took us straight to the King!

MOTHER I knew it –

What did the King say?

JILL He made Jack a prince at once!

Cheers from Mother and fairies

JACK So we want you all to come to the wedding!

A happy moo is heard

ALL *(except Jill)*   Claribelle!

Claribelle comes in with the Old Lady

JACK   This is the one thing I wanted to make me completely happy!

MOTHER   My own sweet Claribelle!

And how well you look – and so plump!

Claribelle moos in Mother's ear

MOTHER   No! Are you really? How lovely for you… when?… Oh, about April?… Yes, of course I'll be there.

JACK *(to Old Lady)*   Thank you a hundred times for being so good to Claribelle. I'd like to buy her back from you. I'll give you any amount of money – I'm ever so rich now.

Claribelle sits down in surprise

OLD LADY No! You gave her to me when I was poor and lonely. Now I give her back, in happiness, to you.

Now that you have your heart's desire, my work is done.

Old Lady drops her cloak. She is a fairy

ALL A fairy!

FAIRY OLD LADY My blessing on you all. Learn to enjoy small, humble gifts.

Take – and give – gladly.

Help the poor, the sick and the lonely to smile through clouds and sunshine too.

So may you learn to love one another and live –

HAPPILY EVER AFTER!